Ann

First Published: 2023
© text Menna Machreth, 2023
© illustrations Emily Kimbell, 2023

No part of this publication may be reproduced, stored in a retrieval system, or transmitted, in any form, or by any means, electrical, mechanical, photocopying, recording or otherwise without the prior permission of the publisher or a licence permitting restricted copying.

ISBN 978-1-914303-26-5

Published by Llyfrau Broga Books, Whitchurch, Cardiff

www.broga.cymru

Ann

The Radiant Life of Ann Griffiths

Written by Menna Machreth
Illustrated by Emily Kimbell

Ann lived with her family in a small village in rural Montgomeryshire.

Their farm was called Dolwar Fach and they were famous for giving everyone a warm welcome.

There were many merry evenings at the farm, where Ann's friends and family would play the harp, dance or play cards and dice.

Ann's father and friends were keen on poetry. Young Ann learnt a lot by listening to them reading their poems aloud and talking about how to write well.

She dreamt of being a famous poet one day.

When Ann was 17 her mother died and Ann had to do much more on the farm.

Selling wool was a good way to make extra money, so Ann would use a spinning wheel - and of course keep an eye on the sheep!

At about the same time, all over Wales many people were joining a new type of religion.

They said that Jesus Christ was the Son of God, and that following what the Bible said would lead to a new life.

Hundreds met regularly in fields or cowsheds to sing songs full of feeling about God.

These people were called Methodists.

When the Methodists first visited the area, people - including Ann and her family - made fun of them. Some even threw stones to keep them away.

But their message, and their lives, appealed to Ann.

After a lot of thought, she joined the new group as she came to believe the same things as they did.

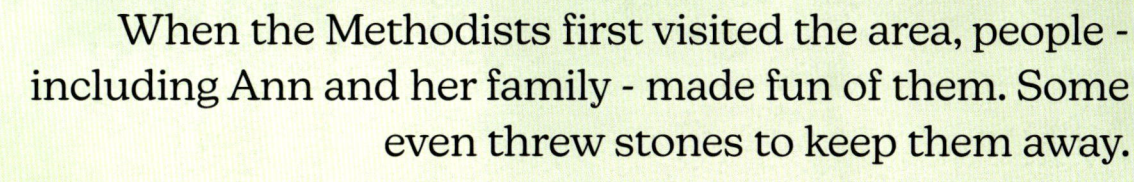

Ann's life was completely changed.

She felt deep joy in her heart when thinking of God.

She often read the Bible to learn more about Jesus Christ, and writing poems and songs was a way for her to describe her feelings.

A maid named Ruth worked at the farm, and she shared Ann's beliefs.

The two were close friends and often walked together over the hill to Bala to meet with other Methodists.

Ruth loved hearing Ann's poems and encouraged her to share them with others.

But Ann didn't want anyone else to see them - she was writing for her own comfort and not for fame.

...wes agoriad, a moeld i hollol gario's ma's. yng yma'r gwaith, y pyrth wedi... ...disgynnodd 'r Hun ddisgynnodd gwedi gorffen... ...ddior fy wh... ...ponhpropp... ...ddau law. ...ysogaethau wedi eu hysbeilio, a'r awdurdodau, garddo ynghyd... ...r ychor draw; y Tad yn siriol a'i... ...ddau law. ...tzyfodiad mawr; dwyn i mewn dragwyddol heddwch. rhwng nef y nef a daear lawr. ...ddyslyd lyfrau tir Arobia. y mae gelynion mwy na rhi'; rho gymdeithas heddychol... ...angau Calfari...

Ann married, and she and her husband Thomas had a daughter called Elizabeth.

The baby was born very weak and died at two weeks of age.

Ann was also ill and died shortly after. She was only 29 years old.

Ruth missed her friend enormously and really wanted other people to hear Ann's lovely poems.

Ruth couldn't write – but she could remember every word and she sang the poems to her husband. He wrote them down as a small book of songs.

They shared the book with friends and, over time, more and more people wanted to sing Ann Griffiths' songs because her beautiful words touched their hearts.

Soon, thousands and thousands of copies were printed and sold across Wales.

The whole country was singing Ann's words.

mae nrhywydd · wrthych teilwng o fy mynd; er mai o ran, yr wy'n adnabod · rhagoriaeth o nad yw eu cwmni · i'w cystadlu teg o bryd; ar ddeng fod unwaith o gweddog o â Iesu mawr: it o! mil sydd chwng y brynu rhyw thir oer i'w quant i eis, fyng i ei eithiad · tysto bo. rhywgwr o

People still sing her words today in chapels and churches in Wales and beyond.

Some say she is one of Europe's finest religious poets.

Ann, the farm girl from Dolwar Fach, did become famous - thanks to her friend's good memory!

Read about more
Welsh Wonders

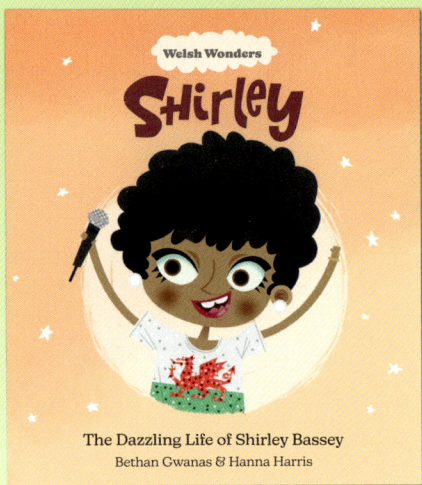

Shirley Bassey
The girl from Tiger Bay whose voice became famous around the world.

Cranogwen
Sarah Jane Rees was a sea captain, prize-winning poet, publisher, and inspiration!

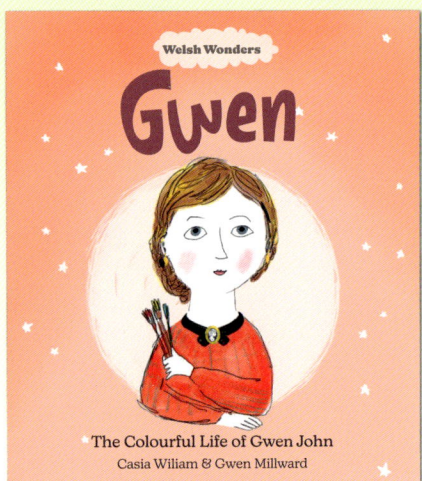

Gwen John
A shy but determined girl who loved to paint and followed her dream of being a famous artist.

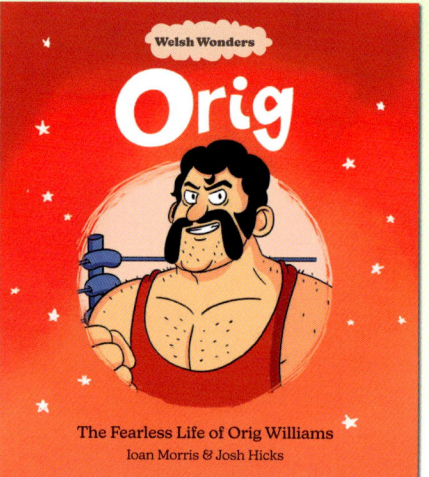

Orig Williams
The tough-guy wrestler with a heart of gold, known around the world as El Bandito!

Aneurin Bevan
Inspirational politician who founded the NHS and changed a nation.

Laura Ashley
Fashion designer who built a business empire from her home in mid Wales.

Coming soon ...

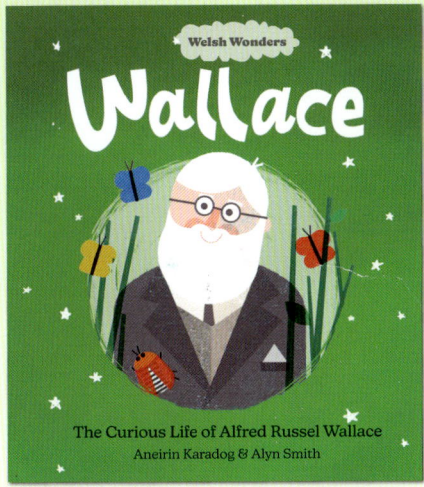

Betty Campbell
The inspirational story of Wales' first Black headteacher, who fought for equality and fairness in education.

Alfred Russel Wallace
The adventurous naturalist who travelled the world and made incredible discoveries.

Find out more about other inspiring Welsh lives – from artists and scientists to people who challenged the way things were and overcame difficulties to achieve their dreams.

broga.cymru